FAMILY LIFE IN
Victorian Britain

RICHARD WOOD

Wayland

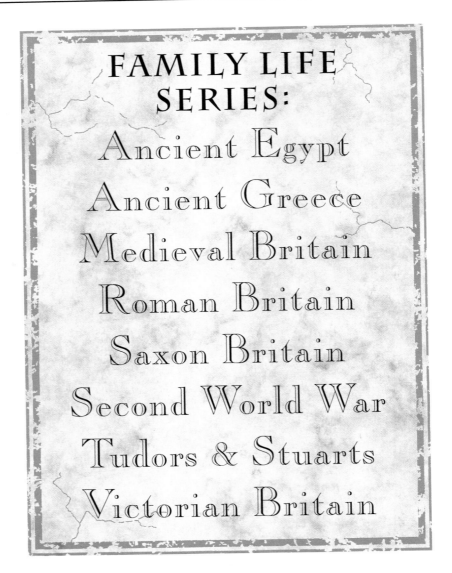

FAMILY LIFE SERIES:

Ancient Egypt
Ancient Greece
Medieval Britain
Roman Britain
Saxon Britain
Second World War
Tudors & Stuarts
Victorian Britain

Series design: Pardoe Blacker Ltd
Editor: Katie Orchard
Production controller: Carol Stevens
Picture researcher: Liz Moore

First published in 1994 by Wayland (Publishers) Ltd
61 Western Road, Hove, East Sussex BN3 1JD, England

British Library Cataloguing in Publication Data
Wood, Richard
Family Life in Victorian Britain. – (Family Life Series)
   I. Title II. Series
   941.081

ISBN 0 7502 1008 7

Printed and bound in Italy by Rotolito Lombarda S.p.A.

Cover pictures: A family having a musical evening, a portrait, and Mrs Beeton's cookery book.

Picture acknowledgements: The Bridgeman Art Library *cover* (Christie's), 20 (Private Collection), 21(Tate Gallery); Dr Barnardo's 9 (top); Mary Evans 4, 12, 17 (bottom), 19 (bottom); Hulton Deutsch 7, 9 (bottom), 10, 11 (bottom), 13 (top), 16, 17 (top), 23 (bottom), 27 (bottom); Billie Love Historical Collection 11 (top), 15, 18 and 19 (top); Archie Miles *cover*; Norfolk Museums Service *cover*, 6, 14 (bottom), 18 (bottom), 22 (bottom), 23 (top), 28, 29; Punch 14 (top); Royal Commission on Historical Monuments in England 13 (bottom); Salvation Army 8; Trinity College Cambridge 26; Richard Wood 5.

With thanks to Norfolk Museums Service for providing pictures from some of their museums.

The remaining pictures are from the Wayland Picture Library.

CONTENTS

VICTORIAN FAMILIES

Queen Victoria was just eighteen when she began her reign in 1837. Three years later, she married her handsome German cousin, Prince Albert. Tragically, their life together lasted for only twenty years, because in 1861 Albert died, probably of **typhoid**. The queen's letters and diaries show her great love for Albert and her concern for the upbringing of their nine children. Stories about the royal family often appeared in newspapers and magazines. For many people, the royal family became a model for the rest of the nation to follow.

The royal family in 1846. Queen Victoria had nine children and became a grandmother when she was only thirty-nine.

A TIME OF CHANGE

Queen Victoria's long reign saw many changes. Britain became the richest country in the world, ruling a powerful **empire** which covered a quarter of the earth. The population increased from nineteen million to thirty-seven million. Towns in particular grew much bigger. People became more **mobile**, thanks to the spread of railways and the use of steamships for transport. Many people enjoyed the benefits of improvements in the standards of health and hygiene, schooling, working conditions and also in home comforts. Some Victorians said that all this change was only possible because of the strong family ties which held people and the country together.

For middle-class families, like the Hirsts of Hull, life seemed comfortable and secure.

IDEALS AND REALITIES

We think of the typical Victorian family as being well fed and happy, with two parents and many children – like the family shown here. In reality, however, family life was not always so happy. Victorian fathers were sometimes cruel and uncaring. Women and children had few rights and often worked long hours. Many poor families lived in filthy, overcrowded rooms with no comfort or privacy. For them, family life was more like prison than paradise. By the 1890s, people worried that family life was breaking down and children were turning to crime.

HOME SWEET HOME

Home life for well-off families was very different from that of poorer families. Middle-class families took great pride in their homes and often had servants to help with the housework. The standard of living was usually very high for such families. Poor families often lived in cramped, filthy conditions. Even these poor families were lucky compared to those who had nowhere to live. Homeless families were sent to a miserable life in the **workhouse.**

Well-off families liked to fill their rooms with ornaments and handicrafts.

WEALTHY HOMES

The large homes of rich families were divided into separate parts. Each part was used by different people or had a different purpose. The top of the house held servants' bedrooms and a nursery where a **nanny** looked after the children. From here their noise would not disturb the adults below. On the first floor were the main bedrooms, and in some houses, a large upstairs sitting-room, like the one in the picture. This is where the mistress and older daughters entertained guests for 'morning' calls. These actually took place in the afternoon, once the cleaning chores were done. Fashionable ladies followed strict rules about what to wear, how long to stay and what to talk about.

The ground floor was the busiest part of the house, with the hall, parlour, dining-room and study. Unlike in a modern house, the kitchen was usually small, dark and hidden at the back. This was where the servants worked, so the family did not often come down there. Sometimes there was a special door covered with green **baize** cloth to keep kitchen sounds and smells out of the rest of the house.

*'How **objectionable** it is . . . when a kitchen door fills the house with unwelcome odours.'*

A Glasgow slum in the 1860s. Notice the barefoot boy, and the washing hanging in the street.

POOR HOMES

'I have seen more wretchedness than I ever supposed could exist'.

For the poor, life was far less comfortable. New homes were built too slowly to house the fast-growing population. In cities, large families often huddled into single rooms or even rat-infested cellars. In Liverpool, conditions were particularly unhealthy. Poor, working-class **labourers** died when they were very young, the average age being only fifteen, compared to forty-five for middle-class people. The average poor family in the 1870s consisted of six people living in just four rooms.

A poor family making brushes at home in Bethnal Green, London. One boy has fallen asleep!

HOME WORK

Poor parents often forced children as young as four to work at home. Although they only earned a few pennies a week, this was greatly needed to buy food and fuel. Some families took in other people's washing. Others did **outwork** for local factories. By working up to fifteen hours a day making brushes or gloves, or sewing shirts and dresses, a family could make about two shillings (10p in today's money) – enough to buy bread and cheese, potatoes and tea. Some families bought food from hot pie shops or baked-potato sellers as they did not have enough time or fuel to cook for themselves.

'Little children are kept up shamefully late if there is work.
Mothers pin them to their knees and give them a slap
on the head to keep them awake.'

These hungry children are waving meal tickets. They could exchange them for free food and drink at a Dr Barnardo's home.

Some people had no fixed homes and wandered from place to place. This gypsy family was lucky to have a smart horse-drawn caravan.

Richer families also worked at home, but not for money. Look again at the picture on page 6. You will see many examples of needlework and crafts. Well-off mothers and their daughters occupied their time by doing handicrafts.

THE HOMELESS

Some poor families had no homes at all. They wandered the streets, sleeping under trees or arches. In 1866, an Edinburgh doctor called Dr Barnado went to London. He found so many abandoned children sleeping rough on the streets that he founded special homes to house and feed them. There was still no family life for them there.

Families who became **destitute** went to live in workhouses. The law said that parents and children, husbands and wives, even brothers and sisters had to be separated from each other in the workhouse. They were only allowed to meet for one hour a week. Very poor people did not seem to benefit from the family values that the Victorians were so proud of!

PARENTS AND CHILDREN

Most Victorians expected to marry, set up home and then start a family. Divorce was very rare and, until 1873, it meant that children would always have to leave their mothers and go to live with their fathers.

Two families together for a wedding party in 1865. Notice the many bridesmaids in long white dresses.

TILL DEATH DO US PART

Poor people often married young, perhaps when still in their teens. Better-off people usually married later, in their twenties or thirties, after a long engagement. A middle-class man would not marry until he could afford a comfortable home with servants for his wife and family.

> *'Marriage is the grand object in life to every young Englishwoman.'*

Road, street etc., and no. or name of house	Name and surname of each person	Relation to head of family	Condition as to marriage	Age	Rank, profession or occupation	Where born
Kent Road	James Biggar	Head	Mar	59	Managing Foreman Joiner Retired	Lanarkshire Glasgow
7 Walworth Terrace	Mary Biggar	Wife	Mar	56		Stirlingshire Carronshore
	Mary Biggar	Daur	Unm	32	House Keeper	Lanarkshire Glasgow
	Hugh Biggar	Son	Unm	29	Foreman Joiner	Do
	John Biggar	Son	Unm	16	Clerk	Do
	Thomas Biggar	Son	Unm	14	Office Boy	Do
	Minnie Russell	Grand Daur		9	Scholar	Do
	Bessie Russell	Grand Daur		7	Do	Do
	Annie Russell	Grand Daur		5	Do	Do
	Margaret McLean	Visitor	Unm	58	Laundress	Stirlingshire Carronshore
	Robert Biggar	Son	Unm	18	Clerk	Lanarkshire Glasgow

Given under the Seal of the General Register Office, New Register House, Edinburgh on   20th July 1978

This 1891 census return for Glasgow shows three generations of the same family living in one small house.

Parents tried to make sure that their children married 'respectable' girls or young men 'with **prospects**'. Their weddings were smart, church occasions. The groom wore a black tailed coat, the bride copied Queen Victoria by wearing a long white dress and veil. Poorer people just wore their ordinary best clothes. Like today, some Victorians did not marry, but it was rare for people to live together and have children without first being married in church.

GROWING FAMILIES

Many people followed Queen Victoria's example and had large families. **Census** figures show that in the 1860s, an average of six children were born to each family. By the 1890s this had fallen to just over three per family, and today it is under two. You can check the size of Victorian families by looking at the census records in your local library or record office. Queen Victoria loved children but was not fond of small babies. She once wrote, 'an ugly baby is a nasty thing'.

Some mothers liked to have a new baby every year and were very proud of their large families. However, many children died in very early childhood because of dirty living conditions and poor medical care.

Mr and Mrs Terry from Greenwich, photographed here with some of their nineteen children.

FATHERS

'Children, obey your parents in the Lord.'

Victorian fathers expected to give orders; their wives and children expected to obey. The law gave men almost total control over their families. Until 1879 a man was allowed to beat his wife, before 1882 he owned all her property and money, and until 1891 he could still lock her up. Many people believed that men were naturally superior to women – more intelligent, wiser and stronger. Some men took advantage of their power, and there were many families with stern fathers, timid mothers and frightened children.

However, most families were not like this. Many were just as cheerful and loving as the happiest families today. Victorian people loved to be photographed with their families. These pictures show the real pride and pleasure that parents took in having a happy family.

Some Victorian fathers gathered their families together every day for prayers and Bible readings.

12

MOTHERS

'A wife's duty is the promotion of the happiness of others.'

Some people think Victorian women were weak and idle with little to do all day except read, sew, drink tea and gossip. In most families, however, this was certainly not true. Even middle-class mothers, who employed servants to do their cooking and housework, had to work hard to organize the home and family.

A father telling stories in the parlour. The fireside was a natural focus for family life.

Most women struggled to raise their families with little help or money. Life seemed to be an endless round of chores. In Scotland, working fathers often helped with housework.

In England, however, most men thought that it was unmanly to do what they called 'women's work'.

In most families, mothers looked after their own children, but in very rich homes, nannies and **governesses** did this job. Rich children even ate their meals upstairs in the nursery and only went down to see their parents briefly before bedtime. Some, like the young Winston Churchill (who later became Prime Minister), felt closer to their nannies than to their mothers.

Children in the day nursery of a large Hampshire house in 1899. Nanny is out of sight!

CHILDREN

'Speak roughly to your little child,
And beat him when he sneezes.
He only does it to annoy,
Because he knows it teases.'

The Victorians were very concerned about how to bring up children. Popular magazines like *Mother's Assistant*, *The Home Friend* and *Family Treasure* were full of advice and practical tips.

Some said that children were naturally good and should be treated kindly to bring out the best in them. Others argued that children were born 'full of wickedness' and should be beaten to make them obedient. 'Spare the rod and spoil the child' (meaning that a child who was not beaten would grow up to be spoilt) was a popular family saying.

Despite all the girls shown here, this Punch *cartoon entitled 'A Son and Heir' suggests that the boy is the only one in the family who counts!*

And see! oh, what a dreadful thing!
The fire has caught her apron-string;
Her apron burns, her arms, her hair —
She burns all over everywhere.

Then how the pussy-cats did mew —
What else, poor pussies, could they do?
They screamed for help, 'twas all in vain!
So then they said 'We'll scream again;
Make haste, make haste, me-ow, me-o,
She'll burn to death, we told her so.'

So she was burnt, with all her clothes,
And arms, and hands, and eyes, and nose;
Till she had nothing more to lose
Except her little scarlet shoes;
And nothing else but these was found
Among her ashes on the ground.

Cautionary tales, like Harriet and the Matches, *showed children what would happen if they were disobedient.*

14

Some children were cruelly treated and in 1889 the National Society for the Prevention of Cruelty to Children (NSPCC) was founded to help them. However, in most families children were loved, though treated rather severely by today's standards. Stories like *Harriet and the Matches* were used by parents to frighten children into doing as they were told.

WORKING CHILDREN

Childhood did not last long for many poor children. They were forced by their parents to work long hours in factories, down mines, as servants or as chimney sweeps. In the country, many children worked in gangs on the land. This work was terribly hard and after 1867 it was against the law for children under the age of eight to do this kind of work.

Girls working in a cobbler's shop, 1865. Some people preferred to employ children because they could pay them low wages.

From the 1830s onwards, many new laws were passed to try to control children's working hours and conditions. After 1870, most children attended school until they were ten years old. This was unpopular with many parents as well as children because it meant a drop in the family income. Even in 1901, the year Queen Victoria died, 300,000 children under ten were still working up to forty hours per week. But in most families, childhood was longer and more pleasant than ever before.

FAMILY GATHERINGS

Middle-class family gatherings were often rather formal occasions. A strong sense of family values was important to the Victorians, so a lot of effort was usually made for family gatherings. Traditional social customs played an important part at these gatherings.

MEALTIMES

Mealtimes gave Victorian families a chance to meet together regularly. Meals were quite formal. Father sat at the head of the table, mother at the foot, and the children sat round the sides. Meals did not start until the youngest child said **grace** to thank God for providing food for the table. In better-off homes, a servant helped to pass the dishes and fill glasses. In other families the older daughters did this job.

Family tea in 1890. Even light meals were usually taken seated round a table.

'The rank which people occupy may be measured by their way of taking their meals'.

Middle-class families ate well. Even a 'plain' family dinner started with soup or fish – herrings were very popular. Meats such as boiled rabbits, roast duck or Irish stew followed. To finish there were puddings, fruit tarts or cheese. If guests were invited, the meal was a much grander affair. There could be six courses, each eaten with separate plates and cutlery.

CELEBRATIONS

Christenings, weddings and funerals were chances for larger family groups to get together. People normally lived quite close to their relatives, but any relations from further away could now arrive easily by train. When someone died, the whole family wore black **mourning** clothes. A widow was expected to wear black for a year, then purple 'half-mourning' for a second year. She even wore black jewellery and wrote letters on black-edged paper during this period.

Nearly all Victorian babies were baptized in church. A christening was an important occasion for the whole family.

Christmas was a happy family occasion. Prince Albert set up a Christmas tree for the royal children at Windsor Castle. Other families copied the idea and soon this became a popular custom all over Britain. Christmas cards and crackers, plum pudding and Christmas cake, and visits from Santa Claus are other customs which were started by Victorian families.

Snapdragon was a popular family game at Christmas time. Brandy was poured over currants in a saucer and set alight. The idea was to snatch the currants from the flames. This could be quite dangerous.

ENTERTAINMENT

'Nothing is more delightful to the feminine members of a family than the reading aloud of an amusing publication.'

You probably have a television, perhaps a video and video games at home, but Victorian families had to make their own entertainment. Most people spent far more time reading than nowadays, and some Victorian books like *Alice in Wonderland* (1865) and *Treasure Island* (1883) are still popular today.

Magazines like *Leisure Hour* and *The Family Home Entertainer* gave ideas for games to play and things to make at home. While older members of the family did sewing or woodwork, younger children could make pictures from shells, feathers, straw or woodchips. No wonder Victorian houses often looked cluttered with so many handicrafts on display!

This box held a table-top version of the popular outdoor game of croquet.

Even quite poor homes often contained an old piano. In the evenings, the whole family would gather to sing hymns or parlour songs like 'Come into the Garden Maud' or 'Home, Sweet Home'. People said that a girl who could not sing and play the piano would never find a decent husband.

FRESH AIR

'Perambulators are dangerous in crowded thoroughfares . . . they are a public nuisance.'

Most Victorians believed in the value of fresh air and exercise for the whole family. The invention of the perambulator (pram) in the 1850s made it possible for even the baby to be taken out of doors. Victorian streets had little traffic. They made an ideal play area for poor children – as long as they looked out for horse droppings! Perhaps they played tag or hopscotch, or kicked around a football made from an inflated pig's bladder. Richer families with gardens often had croquet lawns or tennis courts. Country cricket matches on the village green were popular with both the rich and the poor.

(Above) Home entertainment in 1900. The members of this family have gathered together to play, sing and read to each other.

(Right) Tennis was one of the few outdoor sports which girls as well as boys could enjoy.

FAMILY OUTINGS

I n Victorian Britain, almost half the population went to church every Sunday. In fact, church-going was so popular that some people went several times a week. By the 1850s, most children attended Sunday schools as well.

SUNDAY BEST

'Remember to keep the Sabbath day holy.'

Church provided a chance for everyone in the family to go out together wearing their best clothes. They enjoyed meeting friends to sing hymns and hear sermons. Rich people often had heated family pews at the front. The middle classes paid pew rents to reserve good seats, while poorer people crowded in at the back as best they could. Families normally sat together, but in some Welsh chapels men and women entered by separate doors and sat on opposite sides.

Many churches and chapels needed galleries to hold all the people who wanted to attend services.

THE GREAT OUTDOORS

'A healthy mind in a healthy body.'

On Sundays families were able to escape to the countryside for a change of scene. From the 1840s, many cities provided public parks for people to enjoy free of charge. There were sports to watch, too. These ranged from professional football matches (the Football Association started in 1863) to rowdy cock fights and bare-fist boxing matches. The last two were eventually made illegal.

Queen Victoria was fond of picnics, and from the 1850s more and more people ate meals outdoors in the summertime. One reason for their popularity was that the whole family could enjoy them together. Some people bought picnic hampers, complete with special cutlery and crockery. From the 1870s, ready-made food in tins and jars made picnics much easier to prepare.

Some Victorian picnics were lavish affairs. Notice the bottles of fizzy lemonade laid on their sides.

PERFORMANCES

Many Victorian families must have looked forward to Boxing Day, when the pantomime season began. Parents and children crowded into the gas-lit theatres to enjoy the songs, dances and silly jokes of shows like *Cinderella* or *Jack and the Beanstalk*. Sometimes there would be a fair, or a circus. The children gasped at the dangerous acts of the trapeze artists and lion tamers.

Punch and Judy shows, complete with crocodiles, policemen and sausages, were very popular for children's parties. Music-hall variety shows also became popular from the 1880s. However, most people did not think that these were at all suitable for ladies or children because of their cheeky songs and rude jokes.

By 1900 the first moving films were on show. Despite the silent, jerky pictures and piano accompaniments, these early films must have excited families all over Britain.

(Above) Victorian children could play in traffic-free streets, and this organ grinder soon attracted an audience.

(Left) Punch and Judy shows were popular with Victorian children. You will find the same characters in modern-day shows.

HOLIDAYS

In 1871, three **bank holidays** were introduced to give families a short break from work. Many people had never been further than a day's walk from home. The bank holiday gave them a chance to make a day trip by train to a seaside town like Blackpool or Margate.

Longer breaks from work were unheard of for most people. But many middle-class families now spent a week or two at fashionable 'watering places' like Brighton, Bath or Cromer. Even on the beach, they wore smart, formal clothes. They swam from horse-drawn bathing-machines (like little sheds on wheels) to avoid being seen going down the beach in their bathing costumes. Men and boys usually bathed naked, so they used a separate part of the beach well out of sight of the ladies!

A group of middle-class holiday-makers on Cromer beach in Norfolk in the 1890s.

LOOKING AFTER THE FAMILY

Victorian fathers were legally in charge of their families, but their wives had the important job of running the home. A young housewife called Isabella Beeton discovered that many women had not really been taught how to manage running the household. She wrote articles with helpful ideas, which in 1861 appeared as a book called *Mrs Beeton's Book of Household Management.* It soon became a bestseller and modern versions are still published today.

Mrs Beeton's book was full of useful recipes and advice on running the home.

HOUSEKEEPING

Rich ladies often employed **housekeepers** to organize their large houses for them. More and more middle-class people were trying to copy the ways of the rich. They wanted their rooms spotlessly clean, their food varied and fancy, and their families smart, healthy and well-mannered. Most girls learned how to run a home from their mothers. However, in Victorian times, fashions and ways of doing things, like how to serve meals, were changing fast. New gadgets like gas cookers were becoming available too.

Mrs Beeton's book explained things like how to make up a feather bed, how to keep a marble fireplace clean, how to make shirt collars shiny and how to write invitations among other helpful hints. The book had hundreds of pages of recipes and useful sayings like, 'Clear as you go; muddle makes muddle', and 'A place for everything and everything in its place'.

The well-equipped kitchen, parlour and bedroom of this Victorian doll's house enabled a young girl to practise her housekeeping skills.

Victorian rooms often look muddled to us. Their carved furniture and clutter of ornaments and crafts quickly got dirty from coal fires and were hard to keep clean. One way younger girls could learn about the different jobs of running a house was by playing with dolls' houses, like the one in the picture.

DOMESTIC SERVANTS

Cleaning, lighting and tending the kitchen range were important jobs for the maid. Notice her special apron, kept for dirty jobs.

'Cleanliness is next to godliness.'

Imagine having to look after a home and family with no modern facilities. No hot running water, no bathroom, no fridge, no vacuum cleaner and no washing machine. No wonder better-off Victorian families employed servants!

In 1871, over a third of all British girls aged from twelve to twenty were 'in service'. Some working-class people like coal-miners sometimes had maids, though they were often young relatives who worked for nothing except their keep. Rich families often employed several **domestic** servants, including a butler. In most middle-class homes, however, there was just one servant called a 'maid-of-all-work'. Some maids had a hard life. The lucky ones were treated very well – almost like one of the family.

The maid had to wake up very early. She cleaned and lit the kitchen stove, boiled the kettle, dusted the breakfast room and lit the fire, swept the hall, scrubbed the steps and polished the boots. Then she fried the family breakfast. All this had to be done before she ate her own breakfast! Later in the day there were other meals to prepare as well as the rest of the house to clean, beds to make and perhaps sewing and mending to do.

Victorian knives soon went rusty and needed regular polishing. This was done with powder and a knife board or cleaning machine, like the one shown here.

In poorer families, Monday was clothes washing day. All the girls helped, grating soap into a steaming metal tub and churning the clothes with a wooden stick called a 'dolly'. Later in the week, the clothes were dried, flat-ironed and aired ready to look smart for Sunday. In better-off homes, wash days were less frequent, perhaps only once a month. The family had enough spare clothes to last longer between washes.

By late Victoran times, most towns had piped water and sewers and many families had installed water closets (WCs).

A HEALTHY MIND IN A HEALTHY BODY

'The children of the poor are not brought up but dragged up.'

Mrs Beeton was surprised that children 'reared in the reeking dens of **squalor** and poverty' survived at all. Many did not, and died young from disease or hunger. Even in 1901, perhaps a third of all children were undernourished. Poor girls and boys were noticeably shorter and thinner than those from better-off families.

In some homes, the baby's nursery was also used as a wash place for the rest of the family.

In overcrowded towns, diseases like typhoid and **cholera** spread rapidly. In 1866, 'king cholera', as it was known, killed twenty thousand people. But conditions did slowly improve as Parliament made new laws to clear away health hazards and reduce overcrowding. After 1875, every area had to appoint a Public Health Committee. Its job was to inspect food on sale, provide sewers and clean piped water and dispose of rubbish. By now, families were getting smaller, too, and children were generally better cared for. Despite this, people born in the 1870s expected to live for only forty years – thirty years less than people born in the 1970s.

MEDICAL TREATMENTS

Most families could not afford to pay doctors' fees. Free medical treatment was available, but only to the very poor at the workhouse. Instead, people often consulted the chemist and treated illnesses at home. Adverts for ready-made cures, like Zam-Buk Ointment, Browne's Chlorodyne or Whelpton's Purifying Pills often made absurd claims for what they could do. It was claimed that Whelpton's Purifying Pills, for example, would cure everything from skin disease to sea sickness. Some remedies were quite dangerous. Mothers who gave their babies Laudanum (a powerful drug) to stop them crying, risked poisoning them. Some home-made herbal remedies, like gargling with minty water to cure a sore throat, could be helpful.

This Victorian medical chest was a complete kit for making all sorts of home remedies.

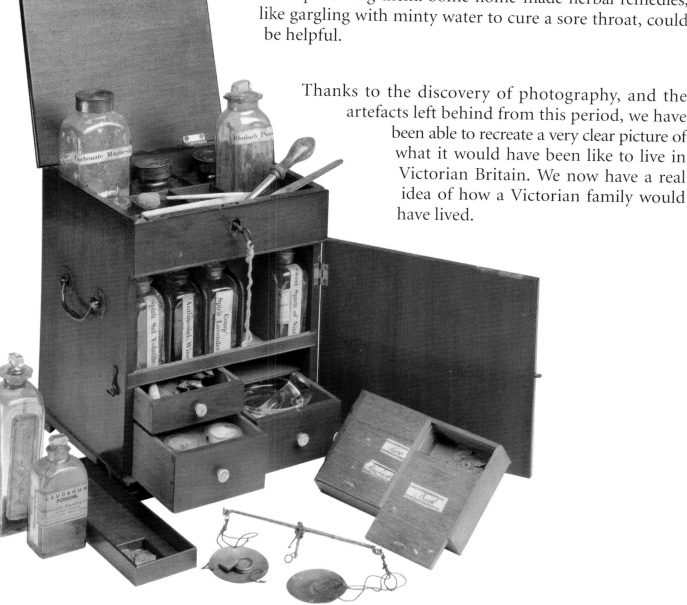

Thanks to the discovery of photography, and the artefacts left behind from this period, we have been able to recreate a very clear picture of what it would have been like to live in Victorian Britain. We now have a real idea of how a Victorian family would have lived.

GLOSSARY

Baize Thick woollen cloth.

Bank holiday An official holiday when banks, shops and factories are closed.

Cautionary Warning.

Census An official count of the population in Britain, carried out every ten years.

Cholera A dangerous infectious disease.

Christening A special church service at which babies are named.

Destitute Having no money at all nor other means of support.

Domestic Belonging to the home.

Empire Several countries all ruled by one government.

Governess A woman paid to teach children at home.

Grace A short prayer said before or after a meal to give thanks for the food.

Housekeeper Someone paid to run another person's home.

Labourers People who work with their hands, usually doing heavy jobs outside.

Mobile Able to move around.

Mourning Expressing sorrow and grief, usually after the death of a close friend or relative.

Nanny Someone who is paid to look after young children.

Objectionable Something that does not meet with one's approval.

Outwork Jobs done for factories in workers' own homes.

Prospects Chances of success in life.

Sabbath The Holy day of rest – Sunday in the Christian religion.

Squalor This usually applies to living conditions and means dirty or unhealthy and unfit to live in.

Thoroughfares Public roads or passages.

Typhoid An infectious disease which causes a high fever.

Workhouses Places where poor people who could not afford to feed themselves had to go. They were very unpleasant and families were often split up.

BOOKS TO READ

Conner, E. *A Child in Victorian London* (Wayland, 1986)

Evans, D. *Victorians: Early and Late* (A & C Black, 1990)

Harper, P. *Finding out about Victorian Childhood* (Batsford, 1986)

Hyndley, K. *Women and the Family* (Wayland, 1989)

Rawcliffe, M. *Finding Out About Victorian Public Health and Housing* (Batsford, 1987)

Wood, R. *A Victorian Street* (Wayland, 1993)

Wood, T. *At the Seaside* (A & C Black, 1992)

PLACES TO VISIT

Many museums and historic houses have displays relating to Victorian family life. Sometimes children's nurseries and servants' rooms are also on show. The places listed below are a very small selection. Find out what is available near you.

Cogges Manor Farm, Cogges, Witney, Oxfordshire OX8 6LA.
A working Victorian farm and house with cooking demonstrations on the range.

D.H. Lawrence Birthplace Museum, Eastwood, Nottinghamshire NG16 3AW.
A small terraced house furnished to show how a poorer family lived.

Museum of Childhood and The People's Story, 42 High Street, Edinburgh EH1 1TG.
Two museums which in different ways give a taste of Victorian family life.

Museum of London, London Wall, London EC2Y 5HN.
A huge and varied collection of household objects from dolls to carriages.

Museum of Science and Industry, Liverpool Road, Manchester M3 4JP.
The sights, sounds and smells of life on the streets of a Victorian city.

North of England Open Air Museum, Beamish, County Durham DH9 ORG.
Ordinary families at home and at work brought to life by interpreters in costume.

Preston Manor, Preston Park, Brighton, East Sussex BN1 6SD.
Retains the atmosphere of a rich Victorian home above and below stairs.

Strangers' Hall Museum, Norwich NR2 4AL.
Recreations of typical rooms from a middle-class Victorian home.

Welsh Folk Museum, St. Fagans, Cardiff CF5 6XB.
Everyday life in Wales displayed through reconstructed houses and room settings.

INDEX

Figures in **bold** refer to illustrations. Glossary entries are shown by the letter g.